The Weight of Air

The Weight of Air

Poems by

M.J. Iuppa

Cover design by Shay Culligan
Cover art: © 2022 Meghan Rose Tonery, *Heart,* color photograph.

ISBN: 978-1-63980-186-2

Kelsay Books
502 South 1040 East, A-119
American Fork, Utah 84003
Kelsaybooks.com

For my husband Peter Tonery
& children,
George D. Marron, Meghan Rose and Nicholas P. Tonery

"And now here is my secret, a very simple secret: It is only with the heart that one can see rightly; what is essential is invisible to the eye."

—Antoine de Saint-Exupéry, *The Little Prince*

Acknowledgments

I am grateful to the editors of the following journals and anthologies where these poems, or earlier versions, first appeared.

Journals:

Anti-Heroin Chic, Amethyst Review (UK), *Autumn Sky Daily, Blueline, The Blue Nib* (Ireland), *Clementine Unbound, The Drabble, Dreams Walking, Dreich 5* (UK), *Eunoia Review* (Singapore), *Foxglove Journal, Freshwater Literary Journal, Front Porch Review, Global Poemic, Here: a poetry journal, Ink Pantry, The Lake* (UK), *Live Nude Poems, Nine Muses Poetry* (UK), *One Art Poetry, The Pangolin Review, Poetry and Place, Prometheus Dreaming, Red Eft Review, SOFTBLOW, Tar River Poetry, Third Wednesday, & The Trouvaille Review.*

Anthologies:

"Safekeeping" in *Le Mot Juste,* Just Poets, 2021
"Face to Face" in *Like Light: 25 Years of Poetry & Prose,* Bright Hill Press, December 2017, edited by Bertha Rogers
"No One Owns the Clouds" in *Lummox Anthology,* 2020, Triolet
"Things Are Not Always What They Seem" *Poetry Leaves,* Waterford Library (Michigan) poetry project, May 2018
"Living Alone in Covid 19 Times" in *Shelter in Place,* Staring Problem Press, 2020

Contents

Plans

Listen. I can't explain what we've been through.
This year of isolation has made us slightly mad.
All of us wishing we could sleep a hundred days
in the crease of a rugged mountain and wake
somehow stronger than before we were given
this wager—
To survive learning the hard way isn't a joke.

We look out our windows, full of whatever
weather is happening, and dream of being
swept up by a steady wind that comes from
far away. We think this is a good plan—we
want to be safe but stand ready with our next
move. We're living behind masks. All anyone
sees is our pupils—those corridors, narrowing
or dilating in response to what we need to do.

Whose plan was that?

Someone who stays up late into the night.
Someone who promises everything will be perfect.
Someone who believes you have what you need.

ONE

Days of Empty Hours

Without a tongue,
the small prayer bell
summons no one

It rains every day—
dismal & persistent—
puddles become harbors

Drifting, briefly—
Birdsong echoes
in ochre light

A dream I tell no one
I tell no one I dream
about this

Barely Morning

It's early. I wake, as I always do, before first light, before
the rumble of the furnace kicks on and gears spin in-

to action, sending warm gulps of air, gushing through
the basement's cloverleaf of heat ducts into the registers

of our dusky rooms of deep cold and sleep. I wake, with-
out waking you, sitting on the edge of our bed, looking

at my socked feet, wondering if they will move in devotion
to me. I stand—feet planted, putting my arms out, with

the gesture of an umbrella opening, and step gingerly in-
to the hall, only to pause at a porthole window that holds

its ransom of winter's blue light reflecting off freshly
fallen snow; and I think hard thoughts about falling

in the depth of this hour, when no one is awake, except
for our gray cat who has found me standing here, at

the turn to the stairs, showing me the way down—
what more could I ask?

Seeking Shelter

All that is lost—momentarily misplaced
  in the stillness of woods filled
with shell-shocked relics—those stone
  footings of barracks left in haphazard
heaps covered in bright green bits of
  lichen and moss—small fires of light
glowing through the clouds' ceiling
  cracks, alighting a path to the frozen
pond tucked inside the deep pocket
  of red osier—an empty room
waiting to be occupied.

Gratitude

This morning I woke, remembering
                                        dream's distant shoals—
sensing the sun's radiation on my neck and shoulders,
          repairing my sallow face—its deep pity for
my seemingly detached feet & hands—how strange it is
          to become a mottled crayfish, single-minded & armored,
ready to scuttle along the rocky ledge of this creek, with its icy
          waters tumbling, over and under, casting phrases
of obscurities—a hundred shades of yellow rise to the surface
          to confuse my sense of direction . . .
                                                      This morning I woke, checking
my body's temperature to see if I were warm-blooded or cold.
          Could I see the familiar or not? Could I lift myself up—
out from under the bedding that swaddles me in another
        winter's sleep?
                                                    This morning, I woke

The Weight of Air

Far from Cliffs of Mohr, I listen to wind, rinsing
through a stand of aspens like rushing

water, while gray & white gulls lift & land as they
follow the tractor that's cultivating the field

next to our farm, like paper hats tossed high in-
to the air, they float until they sail to a sheer

drop, landing lightly on waves of turned earth, in the
same way that they skim the Atlantic's waves

at Hag's Head—the echo of their cries—here & there,
with the weight of air holding every

rock, water, wing in flux, in wind exhaled from the
lungs of God—feeling my strength start

again, as I stand alone in the garden, somehow
shaken by my longing to be in two places at once.

Strandhill Beach in May

—Sligo, 2019

Instantly my breath is lost in this Atlantic air, in
its steady wind swirling around my figure as if
I could be worn down to bits of sand whispering

off the dunes—I look back over my shoulder
to see the Irish sea, muscular and taut, rising
in its infantry of waves, ready to sweep this

expanse of beach—its 15,000 years
of privacy—of barnacles and cockle shells
and God's tears unearthed—those black stones

I pick one by one, only to lose them, with-
out knowing how they fell back to the hard-packed
sand and disappear behind me as if they were

meant to stay here, in my lack of knowledge
of who God is and the impossibility of
keeping what no one else sees.

How It Is

—Galway Bay, 2019

What passes here—unseen
until the noon sky opens
up to an uncharted sea . . .

Cumulus clouds, construed by
sailors drowned, suit a restless
crowd passing over an endless

beach that's eclipsed by a rocky
horizon veering North in-
to fog's silence . . .

Small vacuum of faith, now
apparent in this distance, seized
by a current of wind that exposes

each thing becoming itself before
vanishing to nothing—
like us, learning to look below

the watery mirror of who we are
before there is no sea, or beach,
or ancient rocks to stand on.

How Bright the Moon Shines Tonight

Years past, I consumed an apple seed, tear-shaped
arsenic, in one bite; and since I opened the Empire's
secret tomb, I knew that everything I did from that
point on would turn to stone if I were to reveal what
this seed bore was the music of stargazers, bandits,
paramours—whose lilting tune called to those who
were listening beneath winter's burning dark—the
lure of 7 minutes in Heaven, or the soft nuzzle of
snow that transformed those who had fallen back-
wards into angels in the meadow; and I wanted to go
back to be with them before their warmth disappeared
like low-ceiling clouds erasing this path of moonlight.

I Have Things to Tell You

Before an evening walk at the water's edge, before
we stood on cooling sand and watched a swollen sun

descend through slow-moving clouds; before a path
of golden discs appeared upon stilled water, inviting

us to take our first steps to be embraced by an extra-
ordinary mood that most of us can't put our finger on.

To trust this moment wholly is tidal surge—And, there
we were—mesmerized by this weightless pause, not

listening to any natural distractions, only tethered to
uncompromising beauty that held us in its mystery.

What was it? How does this moment
make us long for love?

No One Owns the Clouds

Lately, when I find myself outside,
and moving slowly, I watch my steps,
careful not to lose my footing in my

preoccupation, which makes me stop
to remember where I'm going, what
small task I need to finish before

coming back into the warmth of
the kitchen, the smells of Sunday
roast, the sounds of logs shifting

their weight in the woodstove.

I pause, knowing I
have lost my center, my point of
purpose, and I look up and see the

trees, naked and unnatural, in winter's
waning light—a silhouette that could
be a mirror reflection, an image of

poverty that's nearly invisible, only
I'll see it deeply, with so many clouds
moving into a stillness—waiting

to comfort me.

Moonlight in the Dead of the Night

How I slide out of bed, without waking
you, doesn't depend on my sloughing off
a skin of sleep—I slip between sheets &
let my numb feet press against the rug's
weave, waiting a few seconds to see if
I can stand in the pewter shine of moon-
light—my body, glowing more alien than
human, posed like a marble angel, whose
eyes are veiled in its single date of life
and death; yet, there is one breath caught
in the purl of the fan, like a small bird
that sleeps in summer's eaves, I hear my
doubts surface in this slow migration,
knowing that I am worse off than you
asleep—knowing I float out of reach,
strangely divine in my aches, no trace
of my footsteps—no telling why this
transformation is mine, alone.

Surviving the Fog

What if I were to wake before the wild
turkey that roosts in the sycamore?

Would I look through dawn's icy haze
to study her slowness to stand, shaking

the cold off feathers & stretching her
neck into that moment of flight—?

A conscious choice—to sail on-
to the snow-covered yard where

no bird or animal has left tracks
to the stillness of woods or orchard

with its toppled trees. I see wind
inside fog, whispering that it's hard

to be pinned down to a semi-colon
of weather, which becomes another

choice, as it begins to snow

There and Not There

In twilight's hazy dark, I walk past our yard's towering sycamore, whose leaves whip-snap in the wind's sudden velocity that picks up everything that's left unattended, including me, without any awareness that I would be taking my first flight—weightless & giddy—my breath stolen; my hands pried from my collar—*Wait—I can't do this!* Not now, or later, even though I've said I wanted to be free from so many objects spinning around me.

Sometimes, the weather calls my bluff.

TWO

Nothing wakes me like rain

pounding its two-fisted anthem on
every surface within earshot and not.

An echo that gallops with a crowd's
commotion, moving in a clatter of tin

elbows and knees, and hands reaching
out for more, then less as the snare of

a truck's headlights on a wet, winding
road finds rain leaping in its down-

shift of wheels, whistling a near
escape, in puddles full of moonlight.

Face to Face

A pine tree leans into wind, hurrying
in oncoming rain.

I keep my head down, walking inside
my steps—certain not to get wet.

The pine tree waves at me, in that come
along-quickly-before-it's-too-late.

                                        After the rain, I
pass the pine, again. This time it stops

me—its boughs dripping quietly,
small splashes of sunlight.

Sinking into the Depths of Noon

Some days, in late May, in the first true heat of Spring, you
can gaze upon the orchard full of blossoms and think of
someone you haven't thought of in years and see that face
as you once memorized it with the tip of your finger, tracing
its light and shade—lips parted in slow, steady breath—full
of pollen, full of bees humming—that song that would eat
itself inside out. You can recall wanting nothing more than
what you cherished briefly, and that face will disappear in the
confidence of your daydream, knowing what no one else knows.

Pink Moon, Sprouting Grass Moon

She couldn't sleep, knowing the seeds she planted
    yesterday in the greenhouse were starting to
tick-tick in thick black loam—starting to sprout

curly tails that turned their shells inside out—&
    those calculating cells divided, unfurling
the blueprint of our garden-soon-to-be

planted without leaving any open spaces—only
    pulsating shadows of so many honeybees finding
their afternoon's work fascinating—and she couldn't

sleep, knowing another season was revving up—
    green and luminous and warm in the scent of
apple blossoms and darkness, and something

out there, tipping over the water can, or stirring
    among the bins in the barn, or the mirror of green
eyes—those green eyes, she just couldn't sleep.

Walking in Fog

In the gloom of a Spring morning,
I feel the slow-moving fog wrap
around me, hiding me inside
these woods where I walk daily
on a path that weaves to the traffic
of worrying, words & thoughts, that
could be accompanied by a storm's
bass & treble notes. I rest, feeling
trapped in wonder, looking up
through the grayness of trees
older than I; and, of rain sifting
down between green branches
that cage me in this small world
perfectly; allowing me to cry
as much as one can cry alone,
without anyone stopping me
from knowing what I can't
survive.

Weathering This

No clouds to speak of—sky, so bright
a blue, that I had to look down as I hiked
along the road's soft shoulder, skirting
bundles of brush left for pick up, and I
spied a small nest in a severed branch
still budding; and beneath it, a robin's
egg, lying cracked open on soft grass, so
bright a blue, that I had to stop & look
closely, hoping for the light touch of
a bird's shadow gliding overhead
like an unexpected cloud.

Living Alone in Covid-19 Times

Day into night into the next day pajamas into night
pajamas into the wash and worn again; but this day
matches top with night bottom; and later on, reverses
it all, when suddenly it's eight p.m. and shadows grow
like tall buildings, even though we live on a farm, not in
the city where you are, and Spring has begun in Prospect
Park, where you run without looking over your shoulder,
until you run home as if someone were waiting for you;
and, just when you open the door, it rains so hard that
you're stunned by its cold touch.

In Need of Company

At what distance does snowmelt reflect the mirror
of windswept apple trees that rise to morning's
apology?
                                          I look and look in-
to a bottomless hour to see my face wrinkling
in the shiver of wind passing over this skin

of water; and bite my lips, wishing I could forget
my dying mother's disbelief when she asked:
Why do you keep your distance from me?

I see myself turning away—confused by her
question. Holding my breath, I wanted
to change the subject to picking out
the right shade of blue.

                                          We couldn't decide if
the sky should be cerulean or azure. We stared
ahead as if it were a comfort. Now, I realize,
a prayer is not the depths of a puddle.

Comparatively, Speaking

My numb feet float in this pool of blue water. Dragonflies flit about, dipping down to sip a drink and disappear without touching my red toenails. My wrinkly feet once belonged to a mummy named Hatshepsut, found wrapped in a tomb, in the Valley of the Kings; and not too long ago, I realized that my feet were her feet that once were anointed in oil, in the Egyptian moonlight that mirrors the face of her wet nurse who was buried in a coffin alongside her sarcophagus; yet, I sit here on the ladder and stir my feet underwater and lament, wishing my feet could travel and trade as they once did, defying men's regard of women with status. You think I should pretend not to know what I know; that I would be better off not protesting too loudly in the ears of men. Certainly, it would make them less suspicious of all the things I tolerate. My numb feet haven't stepped out of this pool of blue water.

Seeing the Sunrise

> *There is only one day left, always starting over: it is given to us at dawn and taken away from us at dusk.*
>
> —Jean Paul Sartre

Soon enough—swallows begin
to stir under the barn's eaves—
one becomes three, becomes five,

filling up twilight's air—so many
blue-black wings scissor-switch
sky to yard—patterns cut in figure

eight precision turning dawn's
pink light into a ramp of sun that
singles out our bedroom window,

our pillows soaked with sleep, and
wakes us to swallows sitting side
by side on a power line, chipping

a tune that echoes until we rise &
look out bleary-eyed upon gardens
we've left undone, knowing we

have another day to finish
what we've started the day
before yesterday.

In Pursuit of Flying

A girl races down the sidewalk, dragging
her stick across bars of sunlight streaming

through the neighbor's slat fence, like
music, her shadow dancing in & out

of time's blank space—that reckless
moment held up to history's sudden

humors, knowing her body could vanish
into deep silence—our hearts hoping

to hear her sail over the crack & land
in a turn—the curve of air, still

swirling, like a sigh, like a cello
trailing its slow exhale.

Mise en Scène

Someone's burning brush, and the smoke
slides across the cornfield into our stand

of swaying pines, where it's caught
in a dance that's weaving a basket

to hold this summer day . . .

Somewhere, too close for comfort,
the sound of rapid gunfire fills the air.

I can't stand that sound.
That *bang, bang*—is never predictable.

I never know if the bullet's coming
wrapped in its blue smoke towards

me—me, who never expected to be
the target, but suddenly I am.

What's happening here?

My world, invaded by every-
day sounds, is coming apart

before my eyes, and I look
again at smoke hanging

on the pine boughs
like dust.

Under a Solitary Sky

The world seems weary in isolation. It complains of not being seen or heard; yet, our meadow, full of goldenrod, will never be as lonesome as crickets simmering in another steamy night. No august stars streak across Ontario, igniting a path to Canada. No one knows where to look. In pines, a screech owl warns that I will die, sooner or later. It depends on who wears a mask. Now the sky thickens into cataract. I look up and realize I am not on this flight—no contrails or flickering jet lights—only clouds converting into mountains that I will never climb. Meanwhile, I lie perfectly still, full of chemicals that make me short of breath, dreaming of a soaking rain.

Obscurity

Standing beneath a clear night sky, the dark
that surrounds you, swallows you, making

you nearly invisible as you look up to see
so many stars flashing their faint light

through phantoms of space, searching for
you sinking in the yard's soft grass, with-

out certainty that you are there, waiting—
everywhere—at once.

Every Word

I trust—gazing into a dewdrop
caught in the white lily's fallen
petal, I see a wealth of sorrow.

Small glimpse into this sphere
of unimaginable terror—of things
I can't even talk about.

The flicker of newsreel—*guerra*
cattiva—faces of strangers who
will not leave me.

The white lily lost its petals in a
downpour—and, this found orb
could be all that I know now.

I look deeply—not wanting this
moment beneath the sycamore
to disappear before my eyes

adjust to daylight.

A Growing Compulsion

So often I am preoccupied with what I am
doing—careful not to let the hoe's blade

take a turn & sever all ties with what is
growing in the garden's raised beds.

My judgment, like my looming silhouette,
makes me nervous. I could be too quick

in this heat that leaves me witless.

                                        I stop & look
behind me to see our scarecrow watching

from the split-rail fence with arms
outstretched—

                              Tipping my head back, I
see the sun has burned a hole in the linen

sky, allowing gray-brown birds to hound
a low-flying hawk with startling speed

until they all disappear in-
to that gaping oblivion—

                               I have never seen what
lives on the other side of sky?

THREE

Triolet: “Things Are Not Always What They Seem”

—after Aesop

Things are not always what they seem
Pine smoke and sealed cells and honeybees
Carrying saddlebags of gold that gleam
Things are not always what they seem
Hidden beneath a mask of decay
Lies the substance of a Queen’s delay
Things are not always what they seem
Pine smoke and sealed cells and honeybees

Captivity

Waking to the gauze-gray gloom of dawn's dissatisfaction, I
exhale—once, for my worn-out sleep that refuses to leave me;
twice, for my numb feet, notwithstanding the labor of walking all

night, without finding a flat rock to rest upon. Most people go to
bed the same way they go to work. Their hearts labor without
complaint; yet, their bodies strain, day after day.

Their sorrow isn't as visible as this morning sky is my boulder.
Lying here, I wonder if I will be able to lift my body to the
next full moon that floats all night in the upstairs window.

Orion

> *I need some older, wiser being to cry to. I talk to God, but the sky is empty, and Orion walks by and doesn't speak.*
>
> —Sylvia Plath

O terrible night—sleepless stars,
that are no longer stars, have sunk
soundlessly to the lake's floor.

Darkness flickers in an unseen
wind, making fallen stars curl
into lonesome buds.

Impossible to imagine this
revival—blossom to blossom
to blossom—ready

to split this skin of sadness.

What Will Be Left, in Leaving?

Strands of hair in a hard bristle brush, an untapped
bottle of body lotion, three gray pills for head-
aches—the lack of time, or is it memory?

Being in a world's constant argument.
What's your position, action, reaction?
Are you a pigeon or parrot? Certainly, you

cluck and coo and squawk in protest of
consonants. Living is a strange parade—
so much confetti left lying on the floor.

Strait of Reflection

Briefly, beauty of a brush-
stroke floats on a bead of

water, whirling cloudy blue
across cold press paper, this

veiled spirit, this lake sky
trembles with the slightest

pressure of light breaking
through—allowing us

to see that speck of a sea-
gull gliding over ruffled

waters—its shapeshifting
shadow guides us, keeping

us from our carelessness.

Ephemeral, lasting—

Beneath our flowering crabapple,
                                        a halo of deep
pink lies loosely around its foot, like
                                        a dropped skirt; un-
disturbed by wind, or a passing creature,
                                        whose dragging belly
clears a path to fallen bird seed, or a sudden
                                        cold rain softening
petals to nothing, as if they were spun
                                        sugar in noon's
sticky heat—a vague knowledge of what
                                        was there—
I stand breathless at the screen, looking
                                        at the wet grass
and leaves dripping, a deeper shade
                                        of green.

Waiting for You in Rain

All the rain I have dreamed,
all of its steadiness, its down-

pour squeezed from swollen
clouds sweeping low—rushing

quicksilver—a thousand *pings*
of light, of dark water

trembling in its blunder—
my words curl up like garden

snails balancing on blades
of new grass.

I am upended—like a bucket
waiting to be picked up by

you, who have wondered where
I've been hiding, until now.

Fair Weather

Freshly turned earth crumbles beneath my fingertips, I
start again, imagining what these new rows will
become . . . First seeds, no bigger than dark specks, sown
in trays that hold the promise of what will sprout
like little green fires, flickering in daylight growing second
by second—seeds not missing a breath, now aching
to straddle this new ground, where I settle them in-
to raised beds; and, as I plant my good intentions, I
smell what these seedlings are before they reveal their plain
selves, whole and upright; and I dream I will make it
to the end of summer to wash them under a rain barrel's spigot
and bring them inside to prepare a meal we will savor
together—if you are my fair weather—and still here with me.

Everyday Gestures

—for my daughter, Meghan Rose

I stand here, before this stove, stirring the pot's
simmering sauce, tasting the tang that drips from
my spoon; feeling the brief poof of steam anointing
my face, a thousand times, in the turn of hours,
wondering if this work in itself is wonder: whose
recipes do I savor these many years, keeping
their secrets in quart glass jars?

I think of life that happens outside of me, what
I can't imagine is going on while I am here, and
you know I am here, and you are there, miles
away, waiting for your gardenia to bloom on
your vanity, in the steam of your bath, some-
thing unexpected and pure, and spicy, like
jasmine, like harmony and grace, like this.

Safekeeping

There is a wooden box sitting on a shelf in the barn.
It's been there for years, collecting thick cobwebs
laced with lost insect wings. I have forgotten what's
in the box. I think I should pull it down from the dark
and open its lid. I think twice. *Do I truly want to know*
what I've been saving? Is it something I couldn't live without;
yet I never needed it? Will I remember the day I put the box
on the shelf and walked away? The wooden box holds
a surprise. One day, you will find it quite amusing.

The Question of Summer

By August, the air grows heavy—everywhere,
a milky haze of overcast—the sun smolders

behind clouds. And here, now
in fields and along roadsides, chicory

sprawls in its barbed wire defense, keeping
invisible boundaries visible.

Lake Ontario settles in its cold spots.
Pines intermittently shift in the day's

slight exhale, releasing puffs of pollen
that drift in golden streaks that stick

unknowingly to our exposed skin
and we glow among the garden's

thick leaf and vine, without knowing
we were picked to answer the question

of summer—how it feels impossible—
a feat of echoes and reflections that defy

us until we lift the burden of beauty,
high over our heads—hypnotic

in its concentration of heat.

Dwelling, Here

At evening, in the lush cornfield alongside our farmhouse,
the mask of light becomes another shade of indigo, and those

green tongues begin to stir, whispering loud, and louder still,
like a crowd of people standing too close to each other.

The loneliness of this hour, even among unison, among luster,
makes me inch closer to this immensity that could swallow me

whole if I walked inside my shoes, inside my skin, without pushing
my way through the tasseled corn that swells with an intoxicating

smell that could make me fall unconscious if I breath too deeply,
like the corn itself, breathing in shadows, surrounding me in

height, hiding me from any world that isn't this world—this other
world that dreams of a life raised up to this deepening light, this

soothing light, this light of dwelling.

Precision of the Minute Hand

The dark of October carries my darkness
in an empty birdcage, in not saying a word
to air that whispers incessantly, just below
my ear—dark face to face—I can't look in-
to the eye of waking in the scent of camphor
& cedar—the fate of keeping something
wrapped in plastic.

For how long?

There, and not there—sad, or is it beautiful
brocade dress—once worn perfectly, and
now who will it fit? Who does this belong
to? Why am I putting it on in the dark?

Today's Sympathy

—Howden Pond, Hamlin NY

Dragonflies adrift in goldenrod
purple asters' bright eyes blink

I could trip over
my desire—dumbstruck, gazing

at these glossy copper wings,
each mirroring the other; even

their tremors appear aloft in this
autumn air, in this pause that

holds no weight to speak of—
on a sunny day, like this

Staying in a Cabin in the Woods in Bristol, NY

When the screen door bangs
shut, pine floors creak with slow
footsteps—silence reshuffles

itself in tattered books
that travel to bed and back
to shelves before morning.

The night sky sails north, high
over mountains whose woods
change in harmonies of rain.

From small windowpanes, I
see a yellow leaf path leading
to its small secrecy.

These woods drift in fog . . .

I open my journal and hear its
spine ache—see its clean page
glow with an unfamiliar light.

On the Brink of Tomorrow

—Howden Pond, Hamlin NY

Leaning on my cherry-switch walking stick, looking
beyond yellow reeds and pearly everlastings, the pond's

depth has shrunk, revealing its puckered banks where
belly tracks of beavers have worn a path to their estate

of young poplars that satisfy their hunger, reducing
trunks to pointed stakes; and at the water's edge,

floating among the reeds, a few stripped branches
wait to be towed to the old den's interior. Yet today,

construction isn't anything more than the wind's
ruffling of yellow leaves and the pond's inky surface.

I am not a reflection here—not a striking shadow,
ready to prove this morning's geometry—only

a set of eyes, wanting to travel without leaving
home—wanting to be standing here, tomorrow.

Fool's Moon, Full Moon

In October, in the shrivel of leaves, the sky
darkens as the fool's moon rises—its face

magnified to a god mask that grins madly
above our threadbare earth spinning in a blur

of land & water, & roads made of clay, like
a curled map lost in a cave that's hidden inside

a mountain known for making its own
weather; no matter what the season predicts.

When this moon begins to tick, the night
stays quiet, listening for an hour to run

out of seconds—waiting to be dispatched
by a squall of snowy expectation.

This Wasn't What I Thought

Not orange leaves, but wings
called wanderer—black-veined brown
found resting on winter's lawn.

Perfectly still—this monarch blends
in. No harm done, in spite of its weight;
its barbed feet anchored to sand.

Left untouched, meaning
this wasn't what I thought—
that I have never truly understood

how insignificant death is until it happens.

Zoom Hour

Sitting in the discomfort of being here, I know you are
listening and not listening; I know you have things on

your mind. I know you are looking at your keyboard,
doing two things at once; wishing the cat would jump

up on your lap, or the dog begging to have its head
scratched, or your 8-year-old, who has been quiet

all morning, pleading outside your workroom for
a cheese & mustard sandwich on soft white bread,

without crusts, and cut into triangles & served
on the red plate that says: *This Is Your Day.*

And, you will shout as we read your lips:
Wait, I am trying to do something. Give me a minute.

I know you're listening for the reassuring sound of
your child's full body thud just outside your door, and

those tiny nails (you really should clip those nails),
dragging against the hardwood floor, in that slow, deep

scratch that takes your breath & proves that I know
you are listening and not listening; I can see your eyes

close, even as I am talking, and I am grateful that you
showed up today. I know you know time is precious.

You don't need to hear it.
Refresh—start, again.

In an Instant Comes a Gust of Whiteness

Walking into the orchard, a foot of fresh snow
conceals the rutted path that will no doubt catch

my toe or heel and throw me off-course as if my
balance were nothing more than an acquaintance

I've forgotten. Even birds are tucked away in
evergreens. I feel their eyes watching me stagger

forward with my shadow leading the way in
this futile exercise.
What is my wish? Is it
to prove that I'm still alive as a Winter after-
noon unfold?

Someone says that he watched me in the orchard.
He says that I was strangely recovered & dancing

on tip-toes—palms against an opaque sky—
dress billowing in the rush of lake air.

He says this in passing in the Post Office to
my husband who knew I was sleeping.

About the Author

M.J. Iuppa was Director of the Visual and Performing Arts Minor Program and Lecturer in Creative Writing at St. John Fisher College (1997–2021.) Since 2002, she has been a part-time lecturer in Creative Writing at The College at Brockport. Starting in 1986, she has been a teaching artist, working with students, K-12, in Rochester, NY, and surrounding area. She was awarded the New York State Chancellor's Award for Excellence in Adjunct Teaching in 2017. She has four full length poetry collections, *This Thirst* (Kelsay Books, 2017); *Small Worlds Floating* (2016) as well as *Within Reach* (2010) from Cherry Grove Collections; *Night Traveler* (Foothills Publishing, 2003); and six chapbooks. She lives on a small farm in Hamlin, New York.

Made in the USA
Middletown, DE
13 August 2024

58708297R10045